SCATTERED

MY JOURNEY THROUGH ADD AND
SELF-DISCOVERY

BRIAN A. FINK

For my father Eric Fink:
My hero, my idol, and my best friend.

CONTENTS

Prologue   1

1. Fragments of Focus   7
   Navigating Childhood Through the Lens of ADD

2. From Shadows to Stars   21
   Navigating Through Darkness

3. Turning Points and New Beginnings   29

4. Noodle Boodle   35

5. The Renaissance Soul   43
   A Symphony of Interests

6. Brothers in Arms   47
   The Unbreakable Bonds

7. Creative Detours   53
   The Unplanned Pauses of Writing with ADD

8. Harnessing Hyperfocus   57

9. Unapologetically, Matt   63

10. Digital Allies   71
    Leveraging Technology to Manage ADD

11. The Company You Keep   77
    Relationships and Their Impact on Well-being

12. Passion and Purpose   85
    Fueling Your Journey

13. Navigating Setbacks and Resilience   91

14. The Road Ahead   95
    Embracing Growth and Uncertainty

About the Author   99

CONTENTS

Preface

PROLOGUE

A JOURNEY THROUGH THE SPECTRUM OF MIND

WELCOME to a journey that navigates the intricacies of attention deficit disorder (ADD), the ebb and flow of motivation, and the resilience of the human spirit. This book isn't just a collection of thoughts or advice—it's a lifeline, a conversation, and a testament to the idea that no matter how scattered or stuck we may feel, there's always a way forward.

I didn't set out to write this book with lofty aspirations of changing the world or dominating the self-help market. I wrote this because I know what it's like to feel lost, overwhelmed, and convinced that success is for someone else. For most of my life, I struggled to believe I could achieve anything meaningful. My mind raced in a hundred directions, my goals felt out of reach, and the whispers of doubt were deafening. But life has a way of teaching us that transformation is possible, even for those of us who feel like the odds are stacked against us.

What exactly is ADD? Attention deficit disorder is often misunderstood, reduced to nothing more than difficulty focusing or being easily distracted. But for those of us who live with it, ADD is so much more nuanced. It's the tendency for our minds to dart between a dozen ideas at once, sometimes igniting bursts of creativity and other times leaving us overwhelmed. It's the struggle to start tasks, not out of laziness, but because the mental clutter makes prioritization feel like climbing a mountain. And yet, it's also the source of unconventional thinking, curiosity, and innovation.

And what about motivation fluctuation? For many, staying motivated is a fairly steady process, but for people like us, it feels more like riding a rollercoaster blindfolded. One moment, the energy to tackle a project is overflowing, and the next, it's completely drained without warning. This isn't a character flaw—it's a reality of how our brains are wired. Learning to manage these shifts is less about forcing consistency and more about embracing the cycles, finding ways to work with them rather than against them.

This book is for the dreamers who feel left behind. It's for the grade-schooler sitting at their desk, feeling like no matter how hard they try, they'll never catch up to their classmates. It's for the young adult watching friends head off to college or launch careers while they're still trying to figure out what they want from life. It's for the thirty-something working tirelessly at a job they don't love, convinced their dreams are too distant to chase. It's for the grandparent who looks back and wonders if it's too late to pursue the life they once imagined. This book is for anyone who's ever felt stuck, scattered, or unsure of their worth.

I wrote this because I realized that the patch-work of my own life—each thread, each venture, and each stumble—has contributed to the complex, colorful medley of my identity. There was a time when I saw my pursuits as failures, believing that not sticking to one thing meant I was incapable or broken. But I've come to understand that each chapter added richness to my story. They weren't failures; they were lessons, skill-building opportunities, and stepping stones that brought me to where I am today.

That realization is what inspired me to begin working on this book. I realized I wasn't alone in feeling this way—this sense of being scattered, this struggle to find a steady path while doubting every choice. And I wanted to write this to connect with others who may feel the same, to show them that being scattered isn't a flaw but a strength.

My inspiration also comes from someone who mirrors my struggles—my daughter. Like me, she has ADD, and like me, she faces the challenges that come with it. I see her fighting battles I know all too well: the frustration of feeling behind, the fear of not being enough, and the constant effort to fit into a world that doesn't always understand how her mind works. I wrote this book for her, to show her that the struggles she faces don't define her. I wrote it to show her that being scattered isn't a flaw —it's a different way of seeing and navigating the world.

But this book isn't just for her. It's for anyone who has ever felt the weight of their doubts and limitations. I've spent years believing that being scattered meant I was lazy or incapable. That's a lie too many of us tell ourselves. Being scattered doesn't mean broken—it means we're wired to see the world from angles others miss. It means we're bursting with creativity and potential, even if it sometimes feels like we can't quite harness it.

This journey isn't about overcoming ADD or motivation struggles in the way people think of "fixing" something. It's about embracing them, learning to navigate the challenges, and finding the strength in what makes us unique. Through personal stories, scientific insights, and practical tools, I'll share what I've learned about coping, adapting, and thriving. This is a book about more than just surviving the challenges of life with ADD or wavering motivation—it's about using those challenges as a springboard to become something greater.

So, to the reader holding this book, whether you're a student, a parent, a professional, or someone still trying to find their path, I invite you to walk this road with me. Together, we'll explore what it means to be scattered, to stumble, to rise, and to thrive. Let's embrace the messiness of life, because it's in the mess that we find the most beautiful stories.

Being scattered doesn't mean we're lost. It means we're capable of seeing the world differently, thinking differently, and, ultimately, achieving differently. This is your invitation to laugh, learn, grow, and discover that being scattered isn't the end of the story—it's the spark of something extraordinary.

CHAPTER 1
FRAGMENTS OF FOCUS
NAVIGATING CHILDHOOD THROUGH THE LENS OF ADD

IN THE EMBROIDERY OF CHILDHOOD, each thread represents a moment, an experience, or a challenge that shapes us. My thread was entwined with the complexity of attention deficit disorder (ADD), creating a pattern that seemed, at times, incompatible with those around me. This chapter delves into those early years, exploring how ADD and motivation, or at times, the stark lack of it, carved a path through my youth, affecting my self-perception, my relationships, and my aspirations.

From a tender age, I harbored a deep-seated desire to make my parents proud. Like any child, I sought their approval, their smiles, and their praise. Yet, despite my earnest efforts, I often felt like I was running a race where the finish line kept moving further away. Now, that's not to say my parents weren't incredibly supportive, because I assure you, they were.

My father, Eric, a chef by trade, worked tirelessly every day. He would come home, often exhausted, yet he never said "no" to sitting down with my brothers, Matt and Shawn, and me to help with homework assignments and studying. His dedication was a constant in our lives, his tired eyes belying a steadfast commitment to our education and well-being.

My mother, a tough little lady from Coney Island, had a mouth that often ran faster than her brain—a trait I inherited and still battle with. She supported us in her unique way, especially in the earlier years of our academic journey. Her approach was different, but the intent was the same—to see us succeed and thrive.

However, despite the cocoon of support from my family, my academic journey felt like a constant uphill battle. My peers seemed to grasp lessons with ease, their achievements setting a standard I struggled to meet. The gap in our academic performances wasn't just a difference; it felt like a chasm, one that whispered incessantly of my inadequacies.

The day I was placed in remedial classes was the day I first tasted the bitter flavor of stigma.

These classes, ostensibly designed to offer support, instead felt like labels that screamed "different" and "less capable." Within those classroom walls, I battled not just with the curriculum but with an internal narrative that questioned my intelligence, my potential, and my worth. The experience was isolating, a solitary journey on a path that seemed to veer away from success and acceptance.

One of my most vivid memories from those years is wrapped in a mix of childhood innocence, unrequited affection, and, strangely enough, Manhattan Clam Chowder. In fourth grade, I was taken out of class every day for language arts and math. The timing escapes me now, but I remember the routine all too well; my "special ed" teacher would arrive to collect a small group of us, leading us away to a separate classroom. This act of being removed, of having someone physically come in and announce it, was humiliating. It set us apart in the most obvious way possible.

One particular day stands out—a day when the "regular kids" stayed behind to prepare for a class-room play based on a book they were reading. We, the "special kids," weren't reading the same book. That divide was just one of the many small reminders that our curriculum, like our placement, was different. My fourth-grade crush, who, in case you were wondering, did not reciprocate my feelings, was cast as the lead. She was animated, commanding, and perfect in my eyes. And I was desperate to be a part of the experience.

I begged. I pleaded. I argued with every ounce of my fourth-grade charm and determination. I wanted to be allowed to read their book and participate in their play. I imagined myself standing on that makeshift stage in that classroom delivering lines with brilliance that would surely win her over. Maybe she'd see me in a new light, or at the very least, we'd share a moment of connection.

Instead, my requests were denied. I wasn't even granted a small role or a chance to stand in the background. When performance day arrived, I sat in the audience, watching her and the other "mainstream" kids act out their roles.

She had this one line—just one—that burned into my memory, though not because it was particularly moving or profound. Her character ordered Manhattan Clam Chowder; that's it—the sum-total of what stuck with me from fourth grade: the sting of being excluded, an unreciprocated crush —a recurring theme of my youth, I might add—and the odd specificity of a soup preference.

Looking back, I can't help but laugh at the absurdity of it all. The memory of her asking for clam chowder and my fixation on that single line feels like the perfect snapshot of where my priorities were at that age. But on a deeper level, it's also an example of how ADD shaped my experiences. My mind didn't hold on to the academic parts of the day—the lessons, the details of the book, or even the overarching plot of the play. Instead, it latched onto the emotional weight of that moment: the rejection, the embarrassment, and the tiny, seemingly insignificant details that made it all so vivid.

That experience wasn't just about being left out of a play. It was a microcosm of what it felt like to be constantly on the outside looking in, to feel "less than" while trying so hard to prove otherwise. And yet, despite the sting of exclusion and the misplaced priorities, moments like these helped shape me. They taught me about resilience, about finding humor even in the most frustrating experiences, and about the ways our scattered minds can cling to the unexpected.

If nothing else, I now have a lifelong association between clam chowder and the struggles of fourth-grade romance. And honestly? That feels like an oddly fitting legacy for a moment that was as painful as it was formative.

The gap between the intentions behind these classes and the reality of their impact on me was vast. They were meant to be a stepping stone to catch up, yet they felt more like an anchor, pulling me further from the shores of confidence and self-assurance.

Bullying added a harsher tone to the already challenging melody of my childhood. With each taunt and tease, with each chant of "Stinky-Finky," my insecurities deepened, wrapping around my motivation like a vine and slowly strangling it. The bullies didn't see the turmoil inside me; they saw a target. Their words and actions became a catalyst for a growing sense of unworthiness, further distancing me from my academic pursuits and from those flickers of joy I once found in learning.

This barrage of negativity led to a downward spiral, not just in my academic career but in my attitude and self-worth as well. I developed a poor self-image and, in my confusion and hurt, began to lash out at those around me.

My best friend at the time, Antonio, bore the brunt of my frustrations more often than he deserved. To this day, he remains my steadfast friend, though we were far from the "cool kids" in school. We first met in October of 1994, not long after I moved to a small town called Middlesex, New Jersey. I was eight years old, about to start second grade in a new school—a daunting prospect for any kid. But I managed to make a friend early on, and he invited me to his birthday party. It was at that party, surrounded by kids I barely knew, that I met Antonio. Something about his awkward, skinny frame and shy demeanor resonated with me, and what started as a chance encounter grew into a bond that would span decades.

Antonio was everything I wasn't at the time: short, skinny, and reserved, while I was short (though briefly the tallest kid in fourth grade—an achievement I now warn my tall fourth-grade daughter to enjoy while it lasts), chubby, and loud. Yet, despite our differences, Antonio became my anchor. Unfortunately, my frustrations often found their way to him. My outbursts were unjust, blaming him for the deeds of others or my own missteps. Antonio's only fault was his unwavering loyalty—a virtue I failed to fully appreciate at the time.

Envy gnawed at me, even though Antonio and I shared a similar social standing. I couldn't help but resent his ability to complete assignments with ease, his absence from remedial classes, and his apparent indifference to our lack of popularity. It was a mystery to me how he navigated school life with such composure. What I failed to recognize was that while Antonio might have had his own struggles, they were different from mine. Without the shadow of ADD to cloud his focus, he navigated academic and social challenges with a grace I longed for but could not emulate.

Our friendship, tested by my misplaced anger and jealousy, somehow endured. Antonio's constant presence taught me lessons about loyalty, understanding, and the complexity of friendship that I would carry with me long after those tumultuous school days.

As adolescence beckoned, the shifting sands of my focus revealed a new horizon. The quest for romantic connections began to overshadow my already fading interest in academics. At the tender age of ten or eleven, fueled by the tales and exploits of my brother Matt, four years my senior, the allure of finding a girlfriend captivated my every thought. Firmly entrenched in his teenage years, Matt and his friends often indulged in conversations about girls and other topics that were, to put it mildly, beyond my years. Eager to fit in and earn the admiration of this older crowd, I mimicked their words and aspirations, casting myself in a role I scarcely understood.

This quest for a girlfriend, I believed, would be the salve for my bruised ego. With each rejection, however, my self-esteem didn't just falter; it plummeted into the abyss. Those rejections weren't mere disinterest; they felt like cruel confirmations of my deepest insecurities. The vibrant joy I once found in my hobbies and interests faded, overshadowed by this all-consuming pursuit of affection.

It was fifth grade, and I had it bad for this girl. Sure, I'd had crushes before. Who could forget my Manhattan Clam Chowder-inspired fourth-grade heartbreak? But this time felt different. Maybe it was hormones. Maybe it was my yearning to grow up too quickly. Maybe it was just my overactive imagination. Whatever the cause, this crush had an intensity that overshadowed all the others.

The problem was that our social standings couldn't have been further apart. I was firmly entrenched on the dorkish low rung of the social ladder, while she was everything I wasn't: athletic, popular, and excelling in school. I had the grace of an elephant and a seat in the special ed program. It was the stuff of a one-sided, tragic love ballad if there ever was one.

But I didn't see it that way. No, in my mind, I needed to show her that I wasn't like the other boys in our grade. I was a mature eleven-year-old, seeking love, not fleeting playground infatuation. Delusional? Absolutely. But that's what made my plan so brilliant.

As Valentine's Day approached, inspiration struck. I decided to leave her a chocolate rose and a note on her desk when no one else was in the class-room. With the help of a teacher, I crafted the perfect message—just vague enough to be mysterious, just romantic enough to spark curiosity. I signed it, of course, "Your Secret Admirer."

When the big moment arrived, I placed the rose and the note on her desk and slipped away unnoticed. The reaction was better than I could have dreamed. The girls in the class crowded around her desk, speculating about which of the "cute boys" had left the gift. I played my part perfectly, joking about the "loser" who'd done such a thing, all while feeling like the coolest kid in the room.

If only I'd stopped there. If only I'd let that victory stand. But one thing ADD loves to steal from you is your sense of restraint. Poor impulse control paired with hyperfocus can make a dangerous cocktail, and I drank it in full measure that day.

Somehow, I convinced myself that the rose wasn't enough. She needed a grander gesture—one so bold she'd have no choice but to notice me. That's when the plan took shape, and it involved my mother's watch—a small, elegant timepiece that I decided would be my ticket to her heart. Borrowing it was out of the question; I was stealing it, though at the time I justified it as "borrowing indefinitely."

I confided in a friend about my plan, explaining how I'd leave the watch on her desk as I had the rose and note. Surely, this would cement me as a romantic genius in her eyes. What I didn't count on was my friend betraying me.

After placing the watch on her desk, I went to the bathroom to bide my time, letting the magic unfold. But my "friend" followed me there, grinning as he revealed he'd already told her who had left the watch. Panic set in. Beads of sweat dripped down my face as I returned to the classroom, my heart pounding.

There on my desk sat my mother's watch, and next to it, a folded piece of paper. I opened it, praying for some kind of miracle. Instead, I was greeted with a single word scrawled in large, bold letters:

"NO."

In that moment, humiliation coursed through me like a tidal wave. The rejection wasn't just painful; it was public. My heart sank as the reality of what I'd done settled in. I'd gambled big and lost even bigger, and now I had to face the fallout—not to mention return my mother's watch and hope she wouldn't notice.

Even now, decades later, the memory lingers like a scar. It's a story I laugh about with friends, sure, but the sting of that rejection—and the impulsive choices that led to it—remains a vivid reminder of the challenges I've faced navigating both ADD and the awkwardness of growing up.

This newfound obsession with gaining the approval of the opposite sex consumed me, relegating my academic efforts to the background. My attempts to focus in class were futile; my mind invariably wandered to daydreams that would be more at home in the pages of a pulp romance novel, complete with all the melodrama and, occasionally, the smut.

My journey through these early flirtations with love was fraught with missteps and misunderstandings. It was a time of learning, albeit through a series of comedic errors and heartfelt attempts at connection. Through it all, the lessons learned were vital, shaping the person I would become and highlighting the difficulties of growing up with ADD, where focus can shift as quickly as the winds, and the heart, ever hopeful, leads the way.

While my story is deeply personal, it's far from unique. Statistics suggest that millions are diagnosed with ADD each year, each individual navigating their own complex journey. The latest data suggests treatment options like medication and behavioral therapy offer avenues for managing ADD, but the path is seldom linear. Understanding and addressing ADD requires a nuanced approach, one that recognizes the individual behind the diagnosis.

In the late twentieth and early twenty-first centuries, treatment and recognition of ADD evolved significantly. Medications such as stimulants have been widely used to help improve focus and reduce impulsivity. Behavioral therapies, educational interventions, and support groups have also played crucial roles in helping individuals navigate the challenges of ADD. Yet, despite these advances, the journey for those with ADD remains deeply personal and varied.

These early chapters of my life, marked by a struggle for understanding and acceptance, began to shape an attitude tinged with negativity. The intersection of academic challenges, bullying, and unmet social desires created a narrative in my mind that was hard to escape. It was a narrative that emphasized my differences, highlighted my failures, and overshadowed my potential.

Yet, within these struggles lay the seeds of resilience, empathy, and a unique perspective on the world. This chapter of my life, while filled with challenges, was also the beginning of a journey toward self-discovery and understanding. It was the start of learning to navigate the chaos, find clarity in the complexity, and recognize the strength in my differences.

In the pages that follow, we'll explore how these early experiences were not the end but the beginning. The journey through ADD and motivation fluctuation is a path of continuous learning, adaptation, and growth. Through it all, the discovery of being scattered becomes not just a challenge but an opportunity to discover the true depth of our resilience and the boundless potential within us.

CHAPTER 2
FROM SHADOWS TO STARS
NAVIGATING THROUGH DARKNESS

BETWEEN THE AGES of thirteen and twenty, I journeyed through the deepest, darkest valleys of my mind. It was a battle waged against ADD, depression, and a crippling lack of motivation—a battle that seemed insurmountable. Loneliness and isolation were my faithful companions, their presence a constant reminder of the rift that lay between me and the rest of the world. This period of my life was marked by darkness, one that was punctuated by legitimate attempts to escape it altogether.

My tumultuous inner world was mirrored by my chaotic academic path; not once, but twice, I was expelled from school. Eventually, I found a place where I belonged, albeit in an out-of-district school designated for those labeled with "behavioral issues."

One night, symbolic of those trying times, I sat on the front porch with my father. The world around us was shrouded in the silence of the midnight hour, a silence so profound it seemed to envelop us. As tears streamed down my face, I shared with him my deepest fear—that the prospect of love, of having a family, was forever marred by the specter of my mental health. By then, I had already found myself within the walls of a mental hospital on twelve to fifteen occasions, one of which saw me spending Christmas at the age of fifteen away from home and family.

When you hear the words mental hospital or institution, your mind might conjure up images straight out of *One Flew Over the Cuckoo's Nest*— dark, oppressive, and ruled by cold-hearted authority. For years, that's exactly how they were described to me by people who remembered the old days. But by the time I was committed for the first time in May of 2000, things had changed. While far from perfect, the mental health facilities I experienced were not the stereotypical rat-infested hellholes of the 1960s and 1970s. They had evolved into something more clinical, more structured, and, at times, even dull.

My first experience stands out vividly for many reasons. I was thirteen years old, a cocktail of hormonal chaos, ADD, and social struggles that made every day feel like an uphill battle. The pressure in my life had been building for months, and it finally hit a breaking point. One afternoon, sitting in my therapist's office—a man I had reluctantly begun seeing at my parents' insistence—I told him flatly that I was going to kill myself that night.

To this day, I can't say if I truly meant it or if I just wanted someone, anyone, to take my pain seriously. I had no plan, no specific method in mind, but my insistence was enough to set off alarm bells. Within hours, I was on my way to the hospital.

At first, I was consumed by pride, stubbornly refusing to admit I needed help. But as the gravity of the situation sank in, panic took over. I begged and pleaded with my parents not to leave me there, tears streaming down my face as I clung to what little dignity I had left. Looking back, as a parent myself, I can't begin to fathom what that night was like for them. I imagine their drive home was filled with tears, silence, and an unbearable sense of guilt, but they stayed strong and did what they believed they had to do. Whether I was truly at risk of harming myself or not, I desperately needed help, and they were right to seek it.

By the late '90s and early 2000s, mental hospitals weren't the grim institutions of old, but they weren't exactly resorts, either. Each day followed the same rigid schedule: wake up, attend group therapy, take medications, meet with your care team, repeat. The routine was designed to stabilize us, to help us confront our issues in a safe and structured environment.

But what truly stood out were the moments between sessions, the little fragments of humanity that found their way into those sterile walls. It was in those moments that I found myself getting into fights or—more often—falling in love. Even in a place where the focus was supposed to be on healing, my mind couldn't help but drift toward finding "the one." Romantic delusions, it seemed, were just as much a part of my recovery process as the therapy sessions.

The Christmas I turned fifteen, I found myself back in the hospital. By then, the process had become almost routine, but this time was different. It was a holiday—the biggest holiday of the year, and I was going to spend it in a place filled with strangers.

Both of my parents are Jewish, but my mother, who grew up in foster care, had started celebrating Christmas as a child. It was a tradition she brought into our home, and there was no bigger holiday for us. The lights, the tree, the presents, the laughter, and the overwhelming sense of family spirit defined the season in our house. I often joke that we were so busy stringing

Christmas lights we didn't have time to light the Hanukkah candles.

But that year, instead of being surrounded by family, I was surrounded by depressed teenagers and overworked staff trying their best to make things feel festive. They tried—they really did—but there's only so much cheer you can force in a place like that. The loneliness was palpable, a heavy weight that hung over everything.

It was a Christmas unlike any other, a stark reminder of the path I was on. I couldn't help but feel like I had wasted my life and was heading nowhere fast. While the holiday spirit was nowhere to be found that year, the experience left me with a lesson that has stayed with me; even in our darkest moments, there is room to grow.

Yet, this narrative of despair is but a prelude to the dawn. History is replete with luminaries who traversed through tumultuous youths to emerge as beacons of hope and brilliance. Their journeys, fraught with struggle, serve as a testament to resilience and the potential for greatness that lies within each of us.

Frida Kahlo - Known for her iconic self-portraits and vivid expression of pain and resilience, Frida Kahlo endured a life filled with physical and emotional challenges. After surviving a near-fatal bus accident as a teenager, she faced lifelong health issues and chronic pain. Yet rather than succumbing to her circumstances, Kahlo channeled her struggles into her art, creating works that have resonated across generations. Her ability to transform personal adversity into a legacy of beauty and strength is a powerful reminder that resilience can lead to remarkable creative and personal breakthroughs.

Abraham Lincoln - Revered as one of the greatest U.S. Presidents, Abraham Lincoln faced numerous setbacks and personal tragedies, including bouts of depression. Yet, his resilience in the face of adversity helped shape a nation during its most divisive period, illustrating that leadership and strength can emerge from the crucible of suffering.

Albert Einstein - Celebrated as one of the most brilliant minds in the history of science, Albert Einstein's early academic and professional life was fraught with challenges and setbacks. As a young student, Einstein clashed with the rote-learning methods of the time and was thought by some of his teachers to be lazy and insubordinate. His difficulties in finding a teaching position after graduation led him to work as a patent clerk, a job far removed from the academic recognition he later achieved. It was during his time at the patent office, however, that Einstein developed some of his most groundbreaking theories, including the theory of relativity. Einstein's story is a testament to the idea that early struggles and non-traditional paths can lead to extraordinary contributions and recognition. His journey underscores the potential within each person to transform perceived shortcomings into the very assets that propel them toward greatness.

These stories, while distinct, share a common thread—the journey through darkness can lead to remarkable achievements and profound transformations. They remind us that the struggles of our teenage years, as insurmountable as they may seem, do not define our potential for greatness.

As I navigated my darkest years, the stories of these remarkable individuals offered a beacon of hope. They served as a reminder that the journey through darkness is not an end but a passage—a passage that leads to the discovery of one's own light.

Revisiting that night on the porch, I now understand that my tears were not just born of fear and despair but were also steps toward healing. They marked the beginning of a journey toward acceptance, toward building a future where love, family, and success were not mere dreams but achievable realities.

Let's turn the page on this chapter with a

renewed belief. Our darkest moments are not the entirety of our story. They are merely the backdrop against which we can shine the brightest. Inspired by the journeys of those who have walked before us, we find the courage to continue moving toward the dawn, toward our moment to shine, proving that from shadows, we too can emerge as stars.

CHAPTER 3
TURNING POINTS AND NEW BEGINNINGS

THE JOURNEY toward self-revelation rarely follows a straight line. Mine meandered through a landscape of fleeting jobs, each lasting no more than a season. From the sudsy basins of dish-washing gigs to the nocturnal sweeps at the local Dunkin Donuts, and even a brief, ill-fated foray into the world of green herbal street-corner sales—a venture my brothers joke was my most enduring occupation of that era.

This carousel of employment was another reflection of the turmoil wrought by ADD and mental illness. The descent into social security disability felt like both a safety net and a surrender, a tacit admission of defeat in a society that vener-ates productivity above all else. The stigma attached to mental illness and learning disabilities often paints sufferers as lazy or unmotivated—a gross misrepresentation that couldn't be further from my truth.

Amid this dark sea of uncertainty and loss, a light emerged in the form of Cynthia, a beacon of strength and understanding. Her entry into my life marked the dawn of a new chapter, illuminating the path through the fog of despair. Through her eyes, I began to envision a future where my struggles were not impediments but integral facets of my identity. Cynthia, who has navigated life's storms with a sense of grace despite constant pain due to Cerebral Palsy, has always been a testament to her resilience. Even on days when the pain is so bad that it keeps her confined to our bed, her spirit remains unbroken, her support unwavering. As I write this, her presence beside me is a tangible reminder of the love and companionship that fuels my journey.

Ironically, I met Cynthia in another therapeutic setting. This time, it was a day program—not so different from the structure of an inpatient stay, except that I was free to go home and sleep in my own bed each night. The program ran from eight to five, offering a mix of group therapy sessions, activities, and structured support to help us find stability in our lives.

Cynthia had started the program before me and was already familiar with its rhythms and social circles. By the time I arrived, she had not only adjusted but had also begun to carve out her own space among the other participants. She was confident, well-acquainted with the daily routines, and seemed to have a solid group of friends.

My first impressions of Cynthia were a mix of fascination and confusion. Her constricted voice initially led me to assume, in my ignorance, that she was deaf. It wasn't until later that I learned her speech was affected by cerebral palsy. At the time, I didn't even know what CP was. The Mayo Clinic describes cerebral palsy as "a group of conditions that affect movement and posture, caused by damage to the developing brain, most often before birth. Symptoms appear during infancy or preschool years and vary from very mild to serious."

After a few days in the program, I decided, like with so many things back then, that I wasn't going to stick with it. It felt pointless, overwhelming, or maybe just uncomfortable. I stopped showing up, prepared to walk away entirely. But after some convincing from my family, I reluctantly agreed to return after missing about three days.

When I walked through the doors again, I wasn't expecting much. But then, something happened that changed my entire perspective. Cynthia, who to that point hadn't said a single word to me, walked right up, smiled, and said, "Hey, I missed you!"

Those four simple words hit me harder than I could have imagined. Her gesture was so pure, so unexpected, and so genuine. In that moment, the walls I had built around myself began to crack. It wasn't grand or dramatic, but it was the start of something profound.

From that small, sincere interaction grew a life-long friendship and a love that has endured every trial and test time has thrown our way.

Our march toward marriage was a long one, hindered not by a lack of love but by the cold calculus of bureaucracy—specifically, social security policies. The prospect of merging our benefits threatened the lifeline of our medical insurance, an odd twist that put the price of love beyond our reach. The irony of being barred from marriage due to my inability to secure stable employment was a cruel one, casting a shadow over our dreams.

It was during this period of reflection and resignation that an unexpected call came. My father, leveraging his position at a rehabilitation center for paraplegics and quadriplegics, had secured a lifeline for me—a per diem dishwasher role. Though it promised no stability, it offered a glimmer of hope, a chance to claw my way out of the rut that had defined my existence. This role, seemingly inconsequential, was the first step on a ladder that led to redemption.

Sustained by the partial stability of part-time work, inspiration struck, stemming from my brother Matt's achievements. The path to becoming a Certified Peer Specialist (CPS) was more than just a career choice—it was a calling. A CPS is a trained advocate who uses their lived experience with mental illness or learning disabilities to support and inspire others facing similar challenges. It gave me the chance to transform my struggles into strength and my experiences into empathy, offering hope to those navigating the complex waters of mental health.

After completing state-certified training programs in both New Jersey and Pennsylvania, I was equipped to build meaningful relationships and guide others on their paths to recovery. The role blends elements of mentorship and social work, creating a dynamic and impactful career.

Each day as a CPS is different. One day might involve helping someone with agoraphobia reengage with their community, while another might be accompanying a client to the Social Security office to renew their benefits. At its core, the work is about showing people that they are not defined by their diagnoses. Through shared experiences, advocacy, and compassion, a CPS serves as a living example that recovery and fulfillment are not just possible—they are within reach.

This journey was not undertaken alone. The families of those with ADD and mental health challenges are unsung heroes, navigating the complexities of support with patience and love. Therapy, support groups, and organizations like CHADD (Children and Adults with Attention-Deficit/Hyperactivity Disorder) and NAMI (National Alliance on Mental Illness) offer extensive resources for individuals and families dealing with ADD and mental health issues. From informational articles and workshops to local support groups and helplines, these organizations are invaluable in the quest for understanding and managing mental health conditions.

In retrospect, I am somewhat amazed by the indomitable spirit of change, the inherent potential within each of us to rewrite our narratives. From the depths of despair to the heights of fulfillment, my story is a testament to resilience, a tale woven from the darkest threads and the brightest hues of love, support, and understanding. It's a mosaic not just of my own making but of all those who've walked this path with me—a testament to the light that can be found, even in the deepest shadows.

CHAPTER 4

NOODLE BOODLE

IN THE TAPESTRY of our lives, there are threads that shine with such intensity, their glow remains long after they've been woven through the fabric of our existence. My mother, Natalie, was such a thread—vibrant, unbreakable strand whose life story was a demonstration of resilience, love, and the complexities of human nature.

Natalie's journey began amid adversity. Orphaned at the tender age of eleven, she and her sister were set adrift in the uncertain waters of the foster care system, separated and alone. The absence of a willing family to embrace them and a father battling his own mental health demons painted her early years with strokes of isolation and struggle. Yet, it was these challenges that forged the resilience and strength that would define her.

Battling juvenile diabetes, Natalie faced her health with the same fierce independence and stubbornness that marked her personality. Her life was a constant battle for balance—a balance often tipped by the very human follies of imperfect diet and the elusive quest for exercise.

Opinionated and unfiltered, Natalie's voice was never lost in the crowd. She possessed a vibrant spirit that could light up a room or ignite a firestorm. Her words were her signature, leaving an enduring mark on the hearts and minds of those she touched.

Through my parents' marriage, I witnessed the epitome of love and devotion. Eric and Natalie's bond was a beacon of hope, illustrating the beauty of a partnership rooted in mutual respect and adoration. Their love story was the lens through which I viewed my future, aspiring to one day find a love as profound and enduring.

Of her three sons, I shared a special bond with my mother. Our connection transcended the typical parent-child relationship, enriched by shared interests and moments of simple joy. We found solace in the melodies of the '50s and '60s, shared laughter over games of cards, and found common ground in the stories that unfolded on the silver screen.

Yet, our journey was not without its storms. My adolescence was a whirlwind of poor choices, one of which left a literal scar on the brand-new car my mom cherished. It was a rash act of rebellion that marred more than just the vehicle's surface—it tested the foundation of our relationship and laid bare the weight of my impulses and anger, perhaps driven by my ADD.

About two weeks before my sixteenth birthday, I got into an argument with my mom. What sparked the fight, I can't recall. What I do remember, vividly, is the moment my emotions boiled over. We were sitting in her new car, a Hyundai my dad bought for her—a momentous milestone for my mom. She had gotten her driver's license in her 40s, after years of driving us around without one. Somehow, she had navigated the world as an unlicensed driver, undeterred by the risk. My mom, it seemed, had an extraordinary ability to make the impossible work in her favor.

When she finally earned her license, her first car was a hand-me-down from my aunt and uncle—a gift she was grateful for, but one that quickly ran its course. After it died, my parents were able to get her a brand-new car, and she was ecstatic. I can still picture the joy on her face when she brought it home, proud of what that car represented.

And then I ruined it.

Fueled by anger and poor judgment, I picked up a stick and scratched an obscenity onto the trunk of her beloved car. The moment the words etched into the metal, the weight of what I'd done hit me like a tidal wave. Regret flooded in, followed by fear and panic. I ran into the house, tears streaming down my face, apologies pouring out of me in desperation. I couldn't believe I had hurt her like that, not just by damaging her car but by tarnishing something she was so proud of.

My mom was heartbroken, and rightfully so. My impulsiveness had caused her pain, and I felt the sting of it deeply. That year, my sixteenth birthday came and went without celebration. No party, no gifts—just the heavy lesson of consequences. And honestly, I didn't deserve a birthday that year.

Eventually, though, my mom found it in her heart to forgive me. Her capacity for understanding and compassion had always amazed me. Over time, I earned back her trust. That forgiveness, that rebuilding of our bond, was worth more than any birthday gift. It was a lesson I carry with me to this day—a reminder of the harm unchecked impulses can cause and the healing power of love and forgiveness.

Natalie was the heart of our neighborhood, a maternal figure to many, embodying a polarity that drew people to her. Her open arms and open-door policy created a sanctuary for those in need of understanding or a place to just be. Her acceptance of Cynthia, my inspiration of hope and love, was immediate and unwavering, accepting her into our family with the ease of a natural-born mother.

Despite her health challenges, including a double bypass that marked just one battle in her long war against her own body, Natalie's spirit never wavered. The TIAs and hospital stays became more frequent as the years wore on, yet her resolve remained unbroken.

April 11, 2015, marked the end of her earthly journey, just two days after her sixty-second birthday. The void left by her passing was vast and deep, a chasm that seemed insurmountable. My daughter Samantha, only seventeen months old at the time, was a living testament to the legacy my mother left behind. Named for the daughter Natalie never had, Samantha carries not just her name but her image—a living, breathing reminder of the woman who shaped my world.

A week prior to her passing, we began noticing something concerning—she was leaning to one side. This was not entirely new; she had been experiencing transient ischemic attacks (TIAs) and mini strokes for some time. We had almost grown accustomed to recognizing the signs, but something about this instance seemed different. At the time, Cindy and I were living in a small two-bedroom apartment with my parents. Samantha was just a newborn, and my mom and dad had offered us a haven while I worked to get on my feet financially.

On this particular day, I decided to take her to the local emergency room. My dad, who had been at work, joined us there shortly after. What we learned that day was devastating. My mom hadn't had another TIA as we had initially suspected. Instead, the doctors informed us that her spine was compressing on itself. Without surgery to relieve the pressure, she would inevitably become paralyzed from the waist down.

Fear gripped all of us, but none more so than my mom. The years of battling diabetes and enduring a cascade of health issues made the surgery incredibly high-risk. Yet, the thought of paralysis was even more daunting for her. After much deliberation, she reluctantly agreed to proceed.

The surgery was scheduled for a few days later. During that time, we surrounded her with love and support. Cynthia and I visited her often, as did my brothers and my dad. Friends called with well-wishes. Each visit was a mix of fear and hope, and I made it a point to keep things light when I could, playing cards with her right up until the day of her surgery.

When the time came, I kissed her forehead and

said, "I love you," as they wheeled her away. It was a moment filled with equal parts hope and dread.

The surgery, by technical standards, was a success. The pressure on her spine was relieved, but her body, battered by years of trauma and illness, could not recover. She never woke up. Her organs began to fail one by one, the strain of everything finally proving too much for her.

At midnight on April 11, 2015, my dad burst into our bedroom. His voice was a mixture of urgency and heartbreak as he said, "Let's go, she's dying." The words took a moment to register, their weight sinking in as I scrambled to get dressed.

When we arrived at the hospital, my older brother, Matt, was already there. With a simple shake of his head, my dad and I both knew—she was gone. My dad let out a guttural cry, a sound of pure anguish that I had never heard before and will never forget.

My mom, while small in stature, had always been larger than life—a force of nature who had held our family together through sheer will and love. Now, she lay before us on a hospital bed, an empty vessel. Her spirit, her fire, was no longer tethered to this earth.

I kissed her forehead again, just as I had before the surgery, and whispered, "I love you." It was a goodbye I had hoped I would never have to say, but in that moment, it was all I could offer to the woman who had given me everything.

"Noodle Boodle," as I affectionately called her, was more than just my mother. She was a woman who faced life's trials with a fierce heart and an unwavering spirit. Her story is a vital chapter in my own, a reminder that through the chaos of life, the struggles with ADD and motivation, there exists a throughline of love, resilience, and human connection.

Today, I see my mother's reflection in Samantha's eyes—a reminder that though we may face the darkest nights, the legacy of those we love continues to guide us, illuminating the path forward with the light of their memory.

CHAPTER 5

THE RENAISSANCE SOUL
A SYMPHONY OF INTERESTS

THROUGHOUT THE GROWING shadows of my depression and the relentless grip of ADD, I sought refuge in the sanctuary of creativity—a realm where imagination knows no bounds and dreams take flight on the wings of words. This journey, marked by shifting passions and fleeting endeavors, became my lifeline, a testament to both the challenges and triumphs of navigating life with ADD.

It all began with a simple love for movies—a fascination with the magic of cinema that captivated my young mind and kindled a fire within my soul. From the triumphant underdog spirit of *Rocky* to the comedic escapades of the *Ghostbusters*, each film served as a portal into worlds where anything was possible. This love of storytelling inspired my first foray into writing—a screenplay based on the television series *Dawson's Creek*. In my version, I was the protagonist, a charming cousin of Dawson's, embarking on a summer of love and adventure. With pen in hand, I felt a sense of liberation—an escape from the trials of adolescence into a world of my creation.

Excitedly, I shared my script with teachers, eager to showcase my budding talent. Their reactions were mixed—part admiration for my ambition, part amusement at my youthful naiveté. Looking back, I realize the script was far from perfect, a clumsy attempt at storytelling driven more by raw enthusiasm than skill. Yet, the process ignited a passion that would carry me through the highs and lows of life.

My creative pursuits didn't end there. At twelve, I embarked on another ambitious project—crafting a romantic comedy in which Britney Spears and Sarah Michelle Gellar vied for my affections. It was as audacious as it was amusing, a teenage fantasy brought to life on paper. Writing became my refuge, a way to channel my loneliness and rejection into something tangible. But as my struggles with mental health intensified, the pages remained blank. Creativity, once a vibrant sanctuary, gave way to darker paths.

In my life, I often found myself in a web of dreams, ambitions, and endeavors. Each pursuit, from the grandiose to the fleeting, marked a chapter in my story, fueled by the restless energy of ADD. Hollywood once called to me, its siren song setting me on a path to become a famous actor. When that dream faded, I turned to professional wrestling, chasing glory and championships under the moniker "The MasterMynd." Though brief, my time in the ring taught me the art of storytelling through physicality, leaving me with cherished memories and valuable lessons.

The digital age brought new opportunities. Inspired by a desire to carve out a niche, I launched a YouTube channel, *The Outmatched Gamer*, focusing on video game commentary. Though short-lived, the venture honed skills in video editing, lighting, and camera work—tools I still use today. Real estate beckoned not once but twice, each time presenting a new chapter in my quest for a legacy. Though motivation waned, these experiences underscored an important truth. My myriad of pursuits were not failures but stepping stones, each enriching my life in unexpected ways.

As I reflect, I see that these endeavors, from writing dramatic scripts to riding the adrenaline rush of the wrestling ring, mirror the experiences of many navigating ADD and fluctuating motivation. They reveal a pattern not of scattered ambitions but of exploration and discovery. Each chapter—even those that felt like missteps—added a unique layer to my story. They taught me resilience, adaptability, and the value of embracing the journey, wherever it may lead.

These moments, both large and small, shaped the eclectic path I've walked. From cinematic aspirations to wrestling glory, from teenage fantasies to professional pursuits, every endeavor has enriched my life in ways I couldn't have predicted. Figures like Leonardo da Vinci, whose interests spanned diverse fields, remind me that exploration is not a weakness but a strength. It's a celebration of curiosity, a testament to the beauty of a multifaceted life.

Each chapter of my journey has been a stepping stone, revealing new facets of my passions and resilience. If there's one thing I've learned, it's that life isn't about finding a single path; it's about embracing the journey. And while the destinations may change, the lessons we carry with us shape the story—a story not of scattered ambition but of discovery and growth.

CHAPTER 6
BROTHERS IN ARMS
THE UNBREAKABLE BONDS

LIFE WITH SHAWN and Matt has been a journey filled with highs and lows, defined by moments of pure joy, profound lessons, and occasional missteps. Growing up, Shawn wasn't just my younger brother; he was my shadow, my twin in every way but birth date. Our shared passions for video games and technology meant that our childhood room was less a sleeping quarter and more a command center for every new adventure we embarked upon.

Shawn had this habit of waking up at the crack of dawn to play video games, thinking he was doing me a favor by not waking me. Little did he know, I was only pretending to sleep, half-listening to the beeps and boops of the game and waiting for my turn. This was our unspoken ritual, a delicate dance of give and take, played out in the glow of the television screen.

Our brotherhood faced its trials, none more harrowing than the time I almost left this world too soon. It was Shawn who found me that evening, his quick action and Matt's unwavering support pulling me through the storm and back to safety. That day, our bond was tested, but it emerged stronger, tempered by the fire of crisis.

At that time, my life had settled into a dark, stagnant routine. Days blurred into nights as I spent most of my waking hours at an all-night diner with a group of equally disillusioned friends. We'd sit for hours, chain-smoking cigarettes and nursing endless cups of coffee, lamenting how the world had passed us by. It was like living in an episode of Seinfeld, except I wasn't Jerry—I was George, the guy who never quite had his life together.

I was on social security, living at home, and convinced that this was as far as life would ever take me. My confidence was non-existent, and I saw no path forward, no way out of the rut I had dug myself into.

On one night (morning actually), around 5 a.m., I was sitting alone on the porch, smoking yet another cigarette—a habit I'm proud to say I kicked almost fifteen years ago. As I exhaled, a dangerous thought entered my mind. It wasn't triggered by anything specific; it was just another reckless impulse born out of years of poor decisions and unchecked emotions. Without much thought, I decided that I was done.

I went into the house, grabbed my medicine bag, and emptied it of every pill I could find. There were probably close to 100 pills in total. I swallowed them all in one motion and lay down on my bed, ready to "go to sleep."

The hours passed in a haze. At around 9 p.m., Shawn came into my room. At first, he thought I was sleeping, but when he tried to wake me, I was unresponsive. My eyes kept rolling back into my head, and I couldn't string together coherent words. Panic set in, but Shawn didn't freeze. Instead, he called for Matt. Together, they sprang into action, rushing me to the emergency room.

The next few hours were a blur. I remember bits and pieces—the harsh fluorescent lights of the hospital, the frantic voices of nurses, and the sharp pain of having my stomach pumped. They flushed my system with fluids and monitored me closely. Miraculously, by the grace of God, I came through it without any lasting physical damage.

Emotionally, however, I was forever changed. My brothers had literally saved my life that night. Their love and quick thinking had pulled me back from the brink. In the days that followed, I was overwhelmed by a sense of gratitude—not just for being alive, but for the bond we shared as siblings. Shawn and Matt's actions weren't just heroic; they were a testament to the strength of our brother-hood, a bond that refused to break even under the weight of crisis.

That night, I realized something profound—even in my darkest moments, I was not alone. My brothers reminded me that life, no matter how messy or difficult, was still worth fighting for. They gave me a second chance, and for that, I am eter-nally grateful.

Then there was the Nintendo incident—a misadventure that showcased both my impulsivity and Shawn's unwavering trust. Convincing him that Antonio's family had miraculously gifted us $300, we rushed to buy the console, a lie hanging between us like a dark cloud. This deceit was a low point for me, a glaring example of the impulsive-ness that often accompanies my ADD. Yet, it was Shawn's forgiveness that taught me the true meaning of brotherly love.

As we grew older, Shawn carved his path with a determination and independence that I couldn't help but admire. Moving out on his own, he set a benchmark for what it meant to step into adult-hood. His journey, distinct from mine, was a beacon of what could be achieved with perseverance and courage.

Matt, on the other hand, was the rock in our trio. Despite our four-year age gap, we shared an unbreakable bond, one that was as much about mutual respect as it was about sibling rivalry. Our childhood was a series of wrestling matches and shared obsessions, from Rocky to Ghostbusters, which provided a backdrop to our formative years.

Matt's health challenges never dampened his spirit; instead, they infused him with a resilience that inspired me. He was always there, a constant presence ready to offer wisdom, share a laugh, or deliver a much-needed reality check. His decision to become ordained to officiate my wedding speaks volumes of his character, though he once jokingly (and awkwardly) claimed to have "married his brother" in a bid to impress someone, a story that has since become legendary in our family lore.

The support and guidance I've received from Shawn and Matt have been instrumental in navigating the ups and downs of ADD. They've been my sounding board for every harebrained idea and the calm in every storm. The lessons learned from our time together have shaped me in ways I'm only beginning to understand.

Our story isn't just about the challenges of ADD; it's about the strength found in family, the power of forgiveness, and the unyielding bond of brotherhood. Shawn and Matt are more than just siblings; they're the cornerstone of my existence, guiding me through life's maze with patience, love, and an unwavering belief in my potential.

Thinking of our childhood and the transition into adulthood, I see not just the paths we've walked but the footsteps we've left behind—marks of our trials, triumphs, and the unspoken vows of brotherhood that no challenge could ever break. Shawn and Matt, in their unique ways, have been my protectors, my challengers, and my greatest allies. In the shadow of these giants, I've found my strength, my purpose, and the unwavering love that defines what it means to be family.

CHAPTER 7

CREATIVE DETOURS
THE UNPLANNED PAUSES OF WRITING WITH ADD

MARCH BROUGHT with it the freshness of spring and the promise of productivity for my book. Yet here I am in June, picking up where I left off, another fine example of the unpredictable journey of living with ADD. It's almost poetic, isn't it? Embarking on a project about ADD and falling victim to its whims along the way. If irony were currency, I'd be a wealthy man.

The truth is, ADD doesn't cater to our schedules or respect our deadlines. It strikes with unpredictable timing, turning what was meant to be a few weeks' break into a months-long hiatus. This isn't unique to me; it's a common storyline for many who live with ADD. We often find ourselves riding waves of intense focus and sudden listlessness, navigating a sea that is as unpredictable as it is vast.

Yet, it's crucial to inject a dose of humor into this narrative. Imagine a writer, fueled by bursts of inspiration, sets out to pen a book about his experiences with ADD, only to be sidelined by the very subject he's writing about. It's the kind of irony that could only be appreciated in a sitcom, or perhaps, in a candid, self-aware book about real life with ADD.

In this unexpected journey, there's a valuable lesson about the importance of self-compassion and understanding the natural rhythms of our minds. It's vital to remember that it's okay to take breaks. It's not just okay; it's often necessary. The world won't end if a project takes a bit longer than planned. This is not procrastination; it's an essential part of managing ADD. It's about allowing ourselves the grace to operate according to a pace that suits our mental health and creative needs.

To find solidarity and inspiration in our struggles with time, let us look at the story of Harper Lee and her masterpiece, *To Kill a Mockingbird*. Lee took over two years to shape her initial manuscript into the final, polished novel. During those years, she faced numerous revisions and bouts of self-doubt, but the time she invested paid off. Her novel not only won the Pulitzer Prize but has become a beloved classic, touching the hearts of millions worldwide. Lee's journey underscores the fact that great things often take time, and the creative process cannot be rushed.

This chapter, then, is a nod to all who find themselves in the clutches of creative endeavors, intermittently halted by the ebb and flow of mental focus. It's a permission slip to take the time you need, to understand that every pause and every detour is part of the journey toward completion. Your process, with all its stops and starts, is valid and valuable.

In embracing this perspective, we also allow ourselves to see the humor in our predicaments. There's something universally human about planning one thing and finding ourselves doing another. It's okay to laugh at the quirks of our brains, to share these moments with others, and to continue moving forward, however meandering the path may be.

So, as I resume the narrative of my book after an unplanned hiatus, I do so with a renewed sense of purpose and a gentle reminder to myself and my readers to be kind to your mind, allow grace to permeate your process, and keep a sense of humor close at hand. The journey might be erratic, but it is undeniably ours, and it is beautifully imperfect. Let's cherish each twist and turn, for they enrich our stories and make our final triumphs all the sweeter.

CHAPTER 8
HARNESSING HYPERFOCUS

HYPERFOCUS, a term synonymous with the ADD experience, encapsulates a state of intense concentration capable of propelling individuals toward unparalleled achievements or ensnaring them in its mesmerizing grip.

During my teenage years, hyperfocus manifested as a tumultuous force, often leading me down perilous paths. Impulsivity coupled with an insatiable desire for instant gratification drove me to steal money from my parents and engage in petty theft from stores. In the throes of hyperfocus, consequences were eclipsed by the allure of immediate satisfaction, resulting in actions I would later come to regret. The damage to relationships was profound; my parents struggled to trust me, resorting to elaborate measures to safeguard their belongings. Despite the guilt that gnawed at me afterward, I found it difficult to break free from the cycle of impulsive behavior.

But truthfully, these challenges didn't start in my teenage years—they began much earlier. Poor choices and impulse control plagued me from a very young age, long before I fully understood the consequences. When I was nine or ten, I had a huge collection of wrestling action figures, my pride and joy. I spent hours each day creating intricate story-lines for my wrestlers, filling my room with the echoes of dramatic matches and championship triumphs (at least as intricate as a ten-year-old's imagination could muster). These toys were more than just objects to me; they were a world I built and cherished.

Around that time, I also discovered a deep love for hip-hop music. The most popular song of the year was *Gangsta's Paradise* by Coolio, a raw and emotional anthem about life in the hood—a place far removed from my small suburban town. But while that song was a cultural phenomenon, this story revolves around a track that came out a few years earlier: *This Is How We Do It* by Montell Jordan. I was obsessed with that song. Its rhythm, its energy, and its coolness captivated me in a way that only hyperfocus could.

One day, my older brother, Matt, mentioned that his friend had the song on a cassette tape.

Remember, this was before iPods, streaming platforms, or even CDs in our house. If you wanted to
listen to a song on demand, you needed to own the
physical media. Hearing this, I became desperate to
have that tape. The problem was that Matt's friend
wasn't willing to part with it for free. He wanted
something in exchange—my entire collection of
wrestling toys.

In a fever of hyperfocus and tunnel vision, I
made the deal. Nearly twenty cherished toys were
handed over in exchange for a three-minute
cassette tape. At that moment, I was so consumed
by the need to possess that song that I didn't
consider the gravity of what I was giving up. Only
later, when the thrill faded, did the regret set in. My
once-cherished wrestling figures were gone, and
with them, the joy of countless hours of imagina-
tive play.

It was a hard lesson, one that taught me about
the consequences of letting my impulses take
control. Yet, as much as I'd like to say it was a
turning point, it wasn't. It was merely one chapter
in a long history of impulsive decisions driven by
hyperfocus. Looking back, it's a story that reminds
me how powerful—and sometimes destructive—
the combination of impulsivity and obsession
can be.

Hyperfocus, while distinctive, is often conflated

with obsessive-compulsive disorder (OCD), leading to misconceptions about both conditions. According to the latest DSM (Diagnostic and Statistical Manual of Mental Disorders), hyperfocus refers to an intense concentration on a specific task or topic to the exclusion of others, characteristic of ADD. In contrast, OCD involves intrusive thoughts and repetitive behaviors aimed at alleviating anxiety, with individuals often feeling compelled to perform rituals to manage distress.

Conversely, in recent years, I've embraced a more constructive form of hyperfocus, immersing myself in a diverse array of subjects—from the stock market to real estate. This thirst for knowledge, while sometimes mistaken for distraction, has enriched my life and broadened my horizons. Through hyperfocus, I've acquired a breadth of skills and insights that continue to shape my personal and professional endeavors. However, my propensity to jump from one topic to another has left others bewildered, struggling to comprehend my ever-shifting focus.

Navigating the peaks and valleys of hyperfocus requires self-awareness, discipline, and resilience. By setting boundaries, recognizing triggers, and practicing mindfulness, I've learned to harness the power of hyperfocus while mitigating its potential pitfalls. Practical strategies, such as time management techniques and organizational tools, offer invaluable support in navigating the complexities of hyperfocus.

Elon Musk stands as a testament to the transformative potential of hyperfocus. Despite grappling with the challenges of ADD, Musk has harnessed hyperfocus to revolutionize multiple industries, from electric vehicles to space exploration. His journey underscores the importance of self-awareness and balance in navigating the turbulent waters of hyperfocus.

I'm often reminded of hyperfocus's capacity to both inspire and ensnare. By embracing its nuances and cultivating strategies for harnessing its power, individuals with ADD can chart a course toward greater fulfillment and success. As I continue to navigate the complexities of hyperfocus, I'm guided by the principles of mindfulness, resilience, and a healthy dose of humor.

CHAPTER 9
UNAPOLOGETICALLY, MATT

LOOKING BACK on my journey to self-acceptance, one person who stands out is my brother, Matt—he's what I like to call "unapologetically, Matt." He remains the same person no matter where he is or who he's with, and I've always admired that about him. While I was busy trying to blend in, he was boldly himself, and it made me question why I couldn't do the same.

I used to struggle immensely with feeling comfortable in my skin. To be honest, that feeling still creeps in from time to time. I was embarrassed by my family and the way they acted, always trying to put on a facade to fit in wherever we went. I didn't even know who I was anymore.

But it wasn't until the last few years that I began to peel back the layers of who I thought I should be and discovered the person I truly am underneath. It was a process of trial and error, of stumbling and falling, but with each step, I grew more comfortable with who I was becoming.

One thing that significantly helped me on this journey was accepting my struggles with ADD and depression as part of who I am. Instead of seeing them as weaknesses, I started to view them as strengths that shaped me into the person I am today. They are a part of me, but they do not define me.

The journey of self-discovery and acceptance came from a few different places. As I stated at the start of this chapter, my admiration for my brother Matt and his unapologetic self is something I marveled at and wanted to emulate. But that alone was not enough to get me to accept myself for who I am. There was a time when it felt like everything was falling apart inside me, even though from the outside, things seemed stable.

A few years ago, I had what I would call a meltdown. I don't know how else to explain it. On paper, everything seemed perfect—I had a stable job, I was married to Cynthia, and we had our beautiful daughter Samantha. But despite all that, something inside me felt hollow. I didn't understand it at the time, but I was dying on the inside, quietly, and I couldn't even recognize it. My mood had been getting darker, and I began to feel a deep sadness that I couldn't explain. It was as if I was walking through life with a weight on my chest that no one could see, and I didn't know how to make it go away.

Then, one night, everything hit me at once. I was sitting in front of the TV, mindlessly watching whatever was on, when out of nowhere, I just lost it. I couldn't hold it in any longer. I started to cry, and not the kind of cry where you shed a tear or two—this was different. I cried like I had never cried before, and I kept crying until there were no more tears left, but even then, the sobs wouldn't stop. I couldn't explain it—there was so much pain, so much frustration, and so much confusion in that moment. I was overwhelmed by the realization that I was so unhappy with my life, yet I didn't know how to change it.

I had watched my friends live their lives on their terms, doing "adult things" and following their dreams, while I felt shackled by the weight of expectations—both the ones I'd set for myself and those imposed by the world around me. I still felt like I was trying to fit into some mold that didn't suit me. In that moment, I questioned everything—my marriage, my career, and the choices I had made. I was trapped in a cycle of self-doubt and disappointment, and I didn't know how to break free.

But what happened next was something I will always be grateful for. Amid that breakdown, I realized something important: I had been carrying around years of shame, guilt, and regret that weren't even mine to hold. I had spent so much time trying to fit into a role that wasn't meant for me, trying to be the person everyone expected me to be, and in doing so, I lost sight of who I truly was. It was in that raw, vulnerable moment of despair that I decided I needed to change the narrative. I had to take a step back and start doing some real soul-searching.

With the help of a therapist and the unwavering support of my family and friends, I began to piece myself back together. I realized that it wasn't my ADD or depression that defined me; it was how I responded to them that mattered. I wasn't weak or broken; I was a person who had endured and learned from those struggles. I had been trying so hard to force myself into a box that didn't fit, but in doing that, I had ignored the unique qualities that made me, me. I took time to understand that I didn't have to be anyone else—I just needed to be unapologetically Brian.

Since that time of near disaster, I've had moments of doubt, moments when the darkness of depression crept back in, and times when I've questioned my decisions. But the difference now is that

I approach those challenges with a new perspective. I remind myself that the person I was then doesn't define who I am now, and more importantly, it doesn't define who I will be. I've learned that setbacks are just part of the journey, and through every struggle, I find more pieces of myself that I can embrace.

Today, I accept that I am a work in progress. That meltdown, that moment of crisis, was the catalyst for a deeper understanding of myself. And now, when I look in the mirror, I no longer see a person who is broken. I see someone who is learning to embrace their journey, imperfections and all. I am unapologetically Brian—and that, for me, is enough.

As I embraced my true self, I found solace and inspiration in the stories of others who had navigated their paths to self-acceptance. Anthony Perkins, a renowned actor, grappled with the challenge of concealing his sexuality during an era when societal norms were unforgiving. His journey struck a chord with me, not because of a shared struggle with sexuality, but because I could empathize with the weight of societal judgment and the pressure to conform to expectations.

On the other hand, there was Elton John, whose boldness in embracing his true identity with courage and conviction served as a shining example of authenticity. His journey was a testament to the power of self-acceptance and the liberation that comes from embracing one's true self, regardless of societal pressures or expectations.

These stories taught me that self-acceptance is a universal journey, one that transcends individual experiences and struggles. While our paths may differ, the destination remains the same—to embrace ourselves fully and unapologetically, just as Anthony Perkins and Elton John did in their remarkable ways.

Continuing to work on accepting myself, I feel a weight lifting off my shoulders—a burden of self-doubt and insecurity that has plagued me for years. While I still grapple with moments of neuroticism and insecurity, I am growing more attuned to recognizing these patterns and, perhaps most importantly, learning to laugh at myself.

In a world where vulnerability is often perceived as weakness and self-deprecation as taboo, learning to laugh at oneself can be a revolutionary act. Too often, we are conditioned to hide our flaws and imperfections, to present a polished facade to the world. But in embracing my quirks and idiosyncrasies, I have a newfound sense of freedom and authenticity.

I can't help but think of The Who's iconic rock opera, "Tommy," and the pivotal moment when the titular character smashes the mirror, shattering the trauma and guilt he had carried with him for so long and embracing his true self. Like Tommy, I too am shattering the mirror of self-doubt and insecurity, letting go of the façade I have meticulously crafted over the years.

In doing so, I discover a sense of liberation—a freedom to be unapologetically myself, flaws and all. I am no longer bound by the expectations of others or the constraints of societal norms. I find the courage to embrace my true identity and chart my own course in life.

It is a transformative journey, one that teaches me the power of self-acceptance and the importance of embracing authenticity in a world that often demands conformity. And while the road to self-acceptance may be fraught with challenges and setbacks, the rewards are immeasurable—a newfound sense of confidence, resilience, and inner peace that can only come from embracing oneself fully and unconditionally.

CHAPTER 10

DIGITAL ALLIES
LEVERAGING TECHNOLOGY TO MANAGE ADD

WHILE LIVING WITH ADD, I've discovered that technology can be both a blessing and a curse. The fast-paced advancements in digital tools mean that there's always something new to explore, and by the time I finish writing this book, countless new apps will have emerged. However, I've found a few reliable allies in the digital realm that have helped me manage my ADD more effectively.

Organization and planning have always been challenging for me, but certain apps have become invaluable tools in my journey. Task management apps that allow me to create detailed to-do lists with due dates, reminders, and priority levels have been instrumental in keeping me on track. Note-taking apps with features to categorize tasks, set recurring deadlines, and even share lists with others have also been incredibly helpful. These apps have been a game-changer in helping me manage my daily life.

Staying focused is another monumental challenge with ADD. There are apps designed to improve focus and concentration, often by providing music tracks specifically tailored to help with these issues. Some apps use engaging methods, like growing virtual trees that thrive as long as you stay focused on your tasks. These tools offer small incentives that, surprisingly, can be very effective.

Managing time effectively is also crucial. Time-tracking apps provide detailed reports on how I spend my time on my devices, helping me identify time-wasting activities and make necessary adjustments. Scheduling apps that sync across all my devices ensure I never miss an appointment and help me stay organized.

Taking care of my mental health is just as important as managing my ADD. Meditation apps offer guided sessions that help reduce stress and improve focus, while online counseling platforms connect users with licensed therapists for virtual counseling. Having these resources readily available has made a significant difference in my overall well-being.

On a personal note, reminder apps have been lifesavers. Apps that help me remember to take my medication on time, log each dose, and set reminders ensure I never miss a dose. Quick reminder apps for jotting down ideas or creating shopping lists with location-based alerts have also been invaluable.

Technology has also been a powerful tool for getting my story out there. I create videos on social media to share my experiences and insights. Video editing apps help make my videos look and sound professional, allowing me to connect with a wider audience and share my journey meaningfully.

Social media, though, is a double-edged sword. It's been a fantastic platform for networking and finding like-minded individuals. The validation from likes and positive comments on my photos and videos, while superficial, has been a boost to my self-esteem. However, the toxicity and negativity on platforms like "X" (Formerly known as Twitter) and TikTok can be overwhelming. The constant judgment and negativity can be a real strain on mental health.

Statistics show that social media can have a profound impact on mental health. Studies have found that excessive social media use can lead to increased feelings of anxiety, depression, and loneliness. Conversely, it can also be a source of support and community for those struggling with similar issues. For example, a study by the Royal Society for Public Health found that social media platforms can help raise awareness and provide a space for open discussion about mental health issues.

Despite these challenges, I've found that embracing my true self and sharing my journey has been incredibly freeing. I've grown more comfortable in my skin over the last few years, though I still struggle with insecurity and being neurotic at times. I've learned to recognize when these feelings arise and laugh them off. This self-awareness has given me more control over my life and the choices I make.

Many people are too afraid to laugh at themselves or embrace who they are. This fear holds them back from experiencing the freedom that comes with self-acceptance. In my journey, I've found inspiration in others who have openly shared their struggles and triumphs with ADD and mental health. For instance, actor and comedian Ryan Reynolds has spoken candidly about his struggles with anxiety and ADD. Reynolds has credited his creativity and humor as essential tools in managing his mental health. He uses his platform to encourage others to embrace their quirks and imperfections, highlighting how technology and social media can be powerful allies in this journey.

Another inspiring example is Olympic

swimmer Michael Phelps, who has been vocal about his battles with ADHD and depression. Phelps has shared how therapy and mental health apps have played a crucial role in his recovery and ongoing management of his mental health. By speaking openly about his experiences, Phelps has helped break down the stigma surrounding mental health issues, encouraging others to seek help and utilize technology as a support system.

The power of self-acceptance cannot be overstated. Embracing who you are, flaws and all, is liberating. It allows you to live authentically and make choices that align with your true self. For me, the journey to self-acceptance has been long and difficult, but it has been worth every step.

In the end, finding productive ways to deal with mental health challenges, particularly with ADD, is crucial. Whether through technology, creative outlets, or self-acceptance, the journey is unique for everyone. By sharing my story and the stories of others, I hope to inspire readers to find their path to self-acceptance and mental well-being.

CHAPTER 11
THE COMPANY YOU KEEP

RELATIONSHIPS AND THEIR IMPACT ON WELL-BEING

IN MY JOURNEY THROUGH LIFE, I've learned that the people you surround yourself with can significantly shape who you become. This quote by American entrepreneur, author, and motivational speaker Jim Rohn resonated with me deeply. "You are the average of the five people you spend the most time with." As I reflect on my life, I see the truth in this.

I've been incredibly fortunate to have a supportive family. My brothers, my father, my wife, and my daughter have all been pillars of strength for me. My parents have shown remarkable forgiveness and understanding, especially during my tumultuous teenage years when I would often steal from them or lie constantly. Their unwavering support and willingness to see past my mistakes helped me find a way back to myself.

Antonio, my friend of over thirty years, has been another constant in my life. He has seen me at my absolute best and my worst, and his friendship has never wavered. His loyalty and steadfastness have been a source of comfort and stability, no matter what life has thrown at me.

But not all relationships are as straightforward. Over the years, I've come to recognize the different types of friends in my life and how they impact my well-being. There are those friends who are always there for me, no matter what. They have been by my side through thick and thin, and I know I can count on them for anything. Their unwavering support and love have been crucial in my journey, providing a safe haven where I can be myself without fear of judgment.

On the other hand, I have friends whom I keep at an arm's length. Some of these friendships have lasted many years and have been there for me during my lowest moments. However, they tend to have a negative outlook on life, where everything is always terrible, and the sky is perpetually falling. While they mean well and I love them dearly, their constant negativity can be exhausting and detrimental to my own mental health. Recognizing the need for boundaries has been an essential part of maintaining my well-being.

Then there are relationships that I've had to end to maintain my mental wellness. One such instance comes to mind when I think back to my childhood. My brothers and I used to wrestle with all the kids in the neighborhood. Much like with my wrestling toys, when we would wrestle, we all had characters, stories, and predetermined winners and losers. One day, while wrestling with a kid I didn't know very well, an accident happened. He flipped me onto my arm, and I heard a sickening crack as my wrist broke in two places. I screamed out in pain, and my parents rushed me to the doctor, where they took X-rays and put me in a cast. The next day, the boy who had broken my arm came over to apologize and check on me. I remember thinking that something good had come of a painful situation. From that point on, he and I became fast friends.

But, as life has a way of teaching us, some friendships come at a cost. This same friend would be the one to introduce me to marijuana, and eventually several other drugs, during my teenage years. It started small, just hanging out, getting high, and smoking cigarettes, but before long, we were finding ourselves tangled up in worse habits. From the age of twelve until about sixteen, we were inseparable. Our bond was founded on reckless behaviors, constant searching for new ways to escape our realities.

But there came a point when even his parents couldn't ignore the destruction anymore, and they sent him away to a rehab program. It was hard for me at first. Losing my constant companion, the one person who seemed to understand my chaos, left a hole in my life. But as time passed, I found ways to cope without him. I slowed down on the drugs and found healthier outlets for my pain and frustration. When he came back, things were supposed to be different. We tried to reconnect, but I could already feel it in my bones—nothing had changed for him. He was still the same person he had been before, still living the life I had been trying to escape.

As hard as it was, I knew deep down that if I was going to move forward, if I was going to break free from this destructive cycle, I needed to separate from him completely. Years later, we ran into each other again, and sadly, things hadn't changed. He was still chasing the same dangerous high, taking risks that seemed impossible to break free from. By that time, I had already become a father, and the reality of the situation hit me harder than ever before. I couldn't risk falling back into old patterns, not when I had a child to protect and care for.

I recently learned that he passed away from an unrelated accident. The news hit me hard. It's heartbreaking to have to end relationships, especially when you truly care for a person. But sometimes, those decisions are about self-preservation. It's a painful reality, but one that I've come to accept. Sometimes, the most loving thing you can do for someone, and yourself, is to let go. And while I'll always remember the good moments we shared, I know that cutting ties was necessary for my survival. It's never easy, but in the end, we have to choose our health and happiness, even if it means leaving some people behind.

One relationship that stands out is with my cousin Melissa. She and I are the only ones from our generation in the family who have children, which has brought us closer together. Our kids, close in age, have grown up almost like siblings. Although Melissa is eight years older than me and we weren't particularly close growing up, the past decade has transformed us into best friends. Melissa is the most positive and inspiring person I know. Her energy is infectious, and I aspire to be like her. She's been my advocate, my role model, and my best friend. Melissa's achievements are nothing short of remarkable—she's written books, worked on podcasts, and inspired many, all while ensuring dinner is on the table each night for her family. She's a superhero if there ever was one, and my relationship with her keeps me motivated and on track.

In pop culture, we see numerous examples of how the company one keeps can significantly impact their life, for better or worse. One notable example is the actor Robert Downey Jr. Early in his career, he was surrounded by a crowd that led him down a path of substance abuse and legal troubles. However, once he changed his social circle and surrounded himself with supportive and positive influences, his life took a dramatic turn for the better. His career resurgence and personal recovery are a testament to the power of a positive support network.

Conversely, the tragic story of Amy Winehouse highlights the dangers of negative influences. Despite her immense talent, Winehouse struggled with substance abuse exacerbated by the negative influences around her. Her untimely death serves as a stark reminder of how the wrong company can lead to devastating outcomes.

The relationships we cultivate play a crucial role in our mental health and overall well-being. Surrounding ourselves with supportive, positive people can uplift and inspire us, while negative influences can drag us down. Embracing who we are and setting healthy boundaries are essential steps in creating a fulfilling and balanced life. By learning from the stories of others and recognizing the power of our choices, we can navigate our journeys with greater clarity and purpose.

CHAPTER 12

PASSION AND PURPOSE
FUELING YOUR JOURNEY

PASSION AND PURPOSE are two of the most powerful motivators in life. They give us direction, fuel our ambitions, and provide a sense of fulfillment. For me, my major motivation and passion come from wanting to provide a better life for my wife and daughter, as well as for myself. This drive has helped me overcome many obstacles and continues to inspire me every day.

When I was younger, at the peak of my mental health crisis, people used to say I would never amount to anything. An extended family member once said, "Brian is a sociopath who will spend his life in and out of jails and institutions." Hearing that at a young age had a profound impact on me. Feeling like people had counted me out slowed my development for sure. Those words echoed in my mind, creating a barrier that seemed insurmountable.

My motivation really came when I met Cynthia. Suddenly, I had purpose and someone to love and fight for. The birth of Samantha added to this passion and motivation. I knew that having a family to care for and provide for was something that would keep me grounded. It took some time, and I still hit some speed bumps to this day, but I am determined to give myself and my family the life we've always wanted.

My father was, and still is, the hardest-working person I know. As far back as I can remember, he would wake up early every morning and head to work, no matter the circumstances. Whether he was healthy or sick, exhausted or sleep-deprived, he never missed a day. In my entire childhood and young adult life, I cannot recall a single instance of him calling out from work. He held down two jobs to make ends meet, sacrificing his well-being to ensure our family had what we needed.

Despite his unwavering dedication, there were times when we found ourselves in financial peril. My mom worked part-time on and off, but her primary role was being a stay-at-home mom, raising three boys while my dad provided for us on a cook's salary. Anyone familiar with working in kitchens knows that it's honest, grueling work, but it doesn't pay much. Yet, despite the challenges, my parents ensured that we always had food on the table, clothes on our backs, and even the joy of toys and video games. By all accounts, we were blessed, but as we grew older and times became tougher, the financial strain became more evident.

There were moments when the weight of it all became too much. The electricity would be cut off, leaving us in darkness, and there were several instances when we fell dangerously behind on the mortgage, hovering near foreclosure. As a kid, I didn't fully grasp the gravity of these moments. I didn't understand the immense pressure my dad must have felt, working tirelessly only to see his efforts swallowed by mounting bills. Looking back, I can only imagine the emotional toll it took on him, pouring everything he had into providing for us and still coming up short through no fault of his own.

Those memories have stayed with me throughout my life. They shaped how I view hard work, responsibility, and what it means to provide for your family. While I may not be where I want to be financially yet (and honestly, who ever truly feels like they've made it?). I carry my father's lessons with me every day. His resilience and dedication fuel my determination to ensure my daughter, Samantha, never experiences the hardships we faced.

I'm driven by the desire to give her the stability and security that I know my father fought so hard to provide for us. I want her to grow up without ever worrying about whether the lights will stay on or if we're at risk of losing our home. That motivation pushes me to work harder, to seize every opportunity, and to make sure the fruits of my labor are realized. It's about more than just money; it's about breaking the cycle of struggle and building a life where my family can thrive, not just survive.

My passion for helping others and for sharing my story started when I became a peer specialist. Although I did not stay with it (there's no way to raise a family on that salary, sadly), I learned that my story, while unique to me, had elements and similarities to others. It made me realize that I had felt so alone for so long, but then I saw that others were struggling with similar circumstances. I wanted and still want others to know that they are not alone, and that they too can achieve anything they set their minds to.

There are many stories of individuals who were either late bloomers or found their passion in unique ways. One such example is Stan Lee, who created his first hit comic title, *The Fantastic Four*, just shy of his thirty-ninth birthday. Before that, he had considered quitting the industry but decided to give it one last shot, leading to a career that spanned over six decades and included the creation of beloved characters like Spider-Man, the X-Men, and Iron Man. Stan Lee's story reminds us that it's never too late to find your passion and make a significant impact.

Another inspiring story is that of Vera Wang. Before becoming a world-renowned fashion designer, Wang was a figure skater and journalist. She didn't enter the fashion industry until she was forty years old, proving that it's never too late to pursue your dreams. Her designs have since become iconic, and she has built a successful brand recognized around the world.

These stories of late bloomers and those who found their passions later in life remind us that there is no set timeline for success. Everyone's journey is different, and sometimes, the twists and turns we take lead us to our true calling.

Finding purpose and passion is a journey that can profoundly impact your life. It provides direction, fuels ambition, and offers a sense of fulfillment. By embracing who you are, laughing at your insecurities, and pursuing your passions, you can overcome obstacles and achieve your dreams.

Remember, it's never too late to find your purpose and make a difference. Just look at Stan Lee and Vera Wang—they found their passions later in life and created lasting legacies. You have the power to do the same.

CHAPTER 13

NAVIGATING SETBACKS AND RESILIENCE

SETBACKS AND FAILURES are an inevitable part of life, but how we respond to them can shape our journey significantly. When I was younger, my approach to challenges was fraught with frustration. I struggled with a mindset that saw every setback as a personal defeat rather than a chance for growth. My history was marked by a series of short-lived jobs and abandoned projects. Each instance of constructive criticism felt like a crushing blow, leading me to give up on pursuits that might have otherwise been rewarding.

In those days, resilience was a foreign concept. I didn't have the tools to view obstacles as opportunities for learning. Instead, I was quick to retreat at the first sign of difficulty. This pattern of behavior not only hindered my career progression but also impacted my personal development. It took years for me to realize that setbacks are not a reflection of our worth but rather a chance to refine our approach and gain valuable insights.

Changing my mindset has been a game-changer. I've learned to approach challenges with a different perspective. Now, when I encounter a setback, I see it as a learning opportunity rather than a failure. This shift in thinking has been pivotal in transforming my approach to both work and personal projects. For instance, working on this book has not been without its hurdles. There have been moments when I felt stuck, and the narrative seemed incoherent. In the past, I might have abandoned the project altogether. Instead, I've learned to step away, gather my thoughts, and return with a fresh perspective. This approach not only helps in maintaining my motivation but also ensures that the final product is something I can be proud of.

Currently, my job presents its own set of challenges. Starting with a new company has come with its learning curve. The software is complex, and managing multiple tasks simultaneously can be overwhelming. There are times when I feel the frustration building up, but rather than letting it consume me, I've developed strategies to manage it. Taking breaks, going for walks, or practicing breathing exercises allows me to reset and reflect on what's causing my stress. This methodical approach to handling frustration marks a significant departure from my previous tendencies to react impulsively.

Public figures often face their own set of challenges, and their stories can be a source of inspiration. Consider Oprah Winfrey, who overcame significant adversity to achieve incredible success. Born into poverty and facing numerous personal challenges, Oprah's journey was marked by setbacks and hardships. However, her resilience and determination enabled her to build a media empire and become one of the most influential women in the world. Oprah's story underscores the power of perseverance and the impact of maintaining a positive mindset despite facing overwhelming odds.

Another example is Steve Jobs, co-founder of Apple Inc. Jobs faced significant challenges throughout his career, including being ousted from Apple, the company he helped create. Instead of succumbing to defeat, he used this period to explore new ventures, ultimately leading to his return to Apple and the company's subsequent resurgence. Jobs' ability to adapt and bounce back from setbacks demonstrates the crucial role resilience plays in achieving long-term success.

Resilience is not just about enduring difficulties but about learning from them and growing stronger. It involves adopting a mindset that views challenges as opportunities for improvement rather than as insurmountable obstacles. By embracing this perspective, we can navigate setbacks more effectively and continue on the path toward achieving our goals.

I recognize that the road to resilience is ongoing. Each setback presents an opportunity to practice patience, adaptability, and persistence. It's a process of continually learning and evolving, and it has profoundly impacted my personal and professional life. Embracing this mindset has not only helped me handle setbacks but has also empowered me to pursue my passions with renewed vigor and confidence.

CHAPTER 14
THE ROAD AHEAD
EMBRACING GROWTH AND UNCERTAINTY

LIFE RARELY UNFOLDS the way we expect. As humans, we crave certainty, yet it's often the unexpected twists and turns that shape us most profoundly. Over the last two years, I've faced significant challenges, particularly with my health. Twice, I've been sidelined by Long COVID, missing over a month of work each time.

The first bout came at a pivotal moment—I had just started a new career in real estate. As I struggled with exhaustion and illness, I had to pump the brakes on my goals and reassess what was possible. It felt like a setback that stirred up old feelings of frustration and failure. But this year, the experience was different. While being home for a month was still difficult, it also opened a door I hadn't realized was there. That time allowed me to focus on the creative projects I had dreamed of for years.

I began recording my podcast, a long-time aspiration, and made significant progress on this book. These weren't just distractions—they were opportunities to explore what I truly wanted to do with my life as I move forward in my forties and beyond. That period of uncertainty taught me that setbacks are often disguised opportunities. By embracing the unknown with curiosity rather than fear, I found purpose even in challenging circumstances.

This idea of continuous growth and learning has become central to how I approach life. Staying committed to your goals is important, but flexibility is equally vital. The path to success is rarely a straight line, and adapting to unexpected changes is a skill worth developing. Growth isn't just about reaching a finish line; it's about who you become along the way. Every misstep, every challenge, is an opportunity to learn and evolve.

History is full of examples of people who thrived by adapting to life's curveballs. One such figure is Samuel L. Jackson, who didn't achieve widespread recognition as an actor until he was in his forties. After years of smaller roles and personal struggles, he landed his breakout role in Pulp Fiction, which catapulted him to stardom. His story is a testament to persistence, adaptability, and the idea that success can come at any stage of life.

Stories like his remind me that growth is a continuous process, not a destination.

Taking into consideration all of the experiences I've gone through in life, I realize it's about more than just overcoming my challenges—it's about helping others along the way. Through my podcast, my previous work as a peer specialist, and now through this book, my goal has been to send a message of hope and resilience. We all have the capacity to achieve our dreams, but as the saying goes, it's not a sprint; it's a marathon. The journey requires patience, persistence, and grace. One of my favorite moments in *Batman Begins* captures this perfectly. "Why do we fall down? So, we can pick ourselves back up." That simple wisdom has stayed with me and continues to guide me.

Your legacy isn't just about what you accomplish for yourself; it's about the positive impact you leave on others. I hope this book inspires you to consider how your own story can create ripples that reach far beyond you. Your journey is unique. It may not look like mine, and that's okay. The struggles you face are part of your story, but they don't define you. Resilience, hope, and a willingness to keep moving forward will carry you through.

There was a moment in my life when I felt like I had hit rock bottom. I was at my lowest point, and I truly believed there was no way forward. In that darkness, I attempted to end my life. But then I met Cynthia.

I never imagined that seventeen years later, we'd still be together, raising a beautiful daughter and building a life full of love and purpose. That moment of despair turned out to be a turning point, one that showed me how much I had to live for. If you're reading this and struggling to see the light at the end of the tunnel, know that it's there, even if you can't see it yet.

My story is proof that life can change in the most unexpected ways. And this book isn't just about me—it's about you and the courage you have to keep moving forward. Your story is still being written, and I can't wait to see how it unfolds.

ABOUT THE AUTHOR

Brian A. Fink is a storyteller, mental health advocate, and the creator behind the growing Scattered community. Diagnosed with ADD and having faced lifelong challenges with focus, motivation, and confidence, Brian has turned his personal journey into a mission to uplift others who feel overwhelmed or stuck. His work blends humor, vulnerability, and practical insight— offering readers and listeners alike a sense of connection and hope.

Brian is the host of the Scattered podcast, a weekly show that dives into the realities of living with ADHD, battling imposter syndrome, and finding your purpose one step at a time. Through this platform—and the private Scattered Beta Group—he continues to provide support, community, and tools for others navigating similar paths.

Outside of content creation, Brian is a dedicated husband and father, drawing inspiration from his family and their shared journey. You can connect with him at <u>linktr.ee/BrianFinkScattered</u>.